Transformations

Other poetry collections by John Reibetanz

Ashbourn
Morning Watch
Midland Swimmer
Near Finisterre
Mining for Sun
Near Relations

Transformations

Edited by Don McKay.
Cover photo by Photo 24, Creatas Images.
Cover design by Lisa Rousseau.
Interior design by Brenda Berry.
Printed in Canada.
10 9 8 7 6 5 4 3 2 1

Library and Archives Canada Cataloguing in Publication

Reibetanz, John
Transformations / John Reibetanz.

Poems.
ISBN 0-86492-458-5

I. Title.
PS8585.E448T73 2006   C811'.54   C2006-903466-4

Goose Lane Editions acknowledges the financial support of the Canada Council for the Arts, the Government of Canada through the Book Publishing Industry Development Program (BPIDP), and the New Brunswick Department of Wellness, Culture and Sport for its publishing activities.

Goose Lane Editions
Suite 330, 500 Beaverbrook Court
Fredericton, New Brunswick
CANADA E3B 5X4
www.gooselane.com

To Julie
"in long embracement"

Contents

Narcissus

She had no conversation but the lisps
 the rocks teased out of her
as she slipped mindlessly past them and eased
 herself into the pool.

Yet poor Narcissus, too trusting to think
 the gods would mock him with
a shadow spouse, traced all her lapses
 to his own.

He read dumbness as fluency in a mute
 tongue too rare for ears,
a language of pulsating light whose syntax
 sang beyond his range.

When he reached out to clasp her hand and it
 spilled from his grip, he cursed
his clumsiness and failure to honour
 virgin modesty.

When cool lips rippled up to slake his thirst
 he thought she knew what thirst

was, and would taste the same liquor the kiss
    sent warming through his veins.

He was the first romantic, tricked by nature's
    brilliant mirrorings
into courting a soul of light he wore
    the years out searching for,

and while age drained the colour from his skin,
    and want of any want
but water thinned him to a mist, she kept
    her features and her youth.

Winged Victory

We never speak of hollow defeat
    as though defeat always came round
        packed solid —

as it does to those
    who pack it in, their mouths
        stuffed with earth, unspeakable.

Victory flies beyond the words
    lips of her lost head might mouth
        or lost arms sign,

broken away, skirts trailing
    footless, pulled taut by hollowing air
        no one can breathe.

Marsyas*

— *in memory of Stephen Jones, builder, motorcyclist, raconteur, 1945-2002*

1.

Mortality sucks from its heartrise, long
  before it breathes. Peeking into
the pink-walled cave of our first living room,
  ultrasound catches toothless mouth
going at it with spectral thumb.

                              Newborn
  we're all windpipe, either howling
to pull the stale air from the lungs' deepest
  pockets
              or gulping down freshets
sucked into hollows convulsed by storms
  of tearless sobbing — ins and outs
echoed by the gullet's greedy cycles
  of swig and burp
                          then, at our prime,
by the whole loving body snorting and
  dipping in and out of its mate's.

---

*In Greek mythology, the satyr and shepherd Marsyas picks up a flute that
Athena throws away because piping on it makes her face look ugly. He
masters the art but loses a musical contest when Apollo unfairly proclaims
his own instrument (the lyre) superior because he can sing while playing it.
Apollo then punishes Marsyas for presumption by stretching him from a
tree and flaying him alive, turning the carcass into a lyre or wind harp.

2.
Who has sucked the colour from your flesh,

                                          sucked

  flesh from your skull's escarpment, now
all grey caves yawning under the forehead's
  crest of damp grey scrub?

                          Only a
god could transform a living body to
  this landscape frozen in drifts of
hospital gown and sheet, only a god's
  vengeance would blow heavenly air
through a clear tube into mortal nostrils
  to be transformed

                  to knives,

                        each breath
piercing, slashing the lungs' blood-drenched
                        branchwork.

  What jealous god invades these groves
steeped in the lilt of your Yorkshire tenor,
  and turns their trembling reeds to sticks?

3.

Apollo's wrath

was, if you crossed him, end-
less as his life, the story goes.
He pegged Marsyas to a tree, stripped off
his clothes and unpeeled the clinging
wet suit of skin,

knife a musician's bow,
blood like waves of sound, body one
open wound, the god's performance unmarred
by the carnal instrument's screams.

Freed from its twitching bundle of flesh
and exposed bone

the skin became
a rarer instrument in divine hands:
strung from another branch, it trilled
unearthly descant in the wind

haunted
by sinews tautened

to harp strings.

4.

And you knew in your bones —

                              stilled flutes now, their

    mortal tune fled —

                    what Apollo

loathed in Marsyas. Mouthy trespassers

    both of you, testing the limits

of your mortality, each hallowed wall

    merely a hurdle to be cleared:

goat-footed Marsyas piping his rout

    of revellers along the slopes

of Mount Olympus, splashing wine,

                                pissing

    on consecrated ground; you, black-

leather-booted, your Harley's twin tailpipes

    breaking wind in staccato on

Blue Mountain, "bringing a little action

    to the comatose."

                    Yet, what drove

5.

divine contempt
                over the edge to rage
   wasn't tanked-up lapses (the gods
expect mortals to act like animals)
   but your cold sober raids upon
divine perfection's heights
                        cordoned off with
   razor wire. So Marsyas honed
Apollo's blade by blowing heavenly
   music through lips
                   that sucked on death,
            a mouth
whose white teeth clasped like maggots to
                        brute flesh,
whose tongue stirred with spices
                        sown in manure,
whose palate swilled discharge
                        from pulped, decaying
                        grapes —
         that mouth
piped harmonies which turned Athena's head
   and blushed the ichor in her veins.

6.

If I were a god, I would treat your pride
   to a kinder transformation.
Sooner than flay your lungs to tatters,
   I'd change you, as gods used to do —
there
      at the peak of your defiance (lips
   whistling summer into the north-
wind's frozen breath)
                  hopping from beam to beam
   as if the timbers of the house
you're framing were the strings of a huge harp
   whose pitch and range rival
Apollo's, I would
         change you, shrink you down:
   shorten the already-squat legs
and fit your bantam strut with lift
   by tapering your arms
              to wings.

7.

This tree swallow will do, stubby-legged but
   elegant flyer
               dipping in
and out of the hollow ash with its mate
   all day, cramming impatient mouths
of pink offspring with insects and mealworms
   to be sucked into feather, flight
and song.
           I watch them from a window of
   the house you built us.
                 We can't see deep
   into the tree's hollow, but hear
the fleeting twitter of mouths that today
   are perfectly unstoppable.

Head and Torso of the Minotaur

1. Theseus at the Heart of the Labyrinth

The monster and the sacrifice are one,
the weapon anchored in the skull that bred it.
The first secret the hero has unearthed
disturbs him least — the torso of a woman
charging under the maned, snorting head.
His eye reads all as bestial, takes for proof
ripe breasts made monstrous by the drying blood.
The second will drive dream to sacrifice;
yet, only when their ship ties up at Naxos
does he take in what flickered by too quickly
as he plunged the horn into the skull's fountain.
Beyond the end of Ariadne's silk,
the snout's black nostrils, the jowl's slobbered fur:
eyes — human, hers, and anchored in them, his.

2. *Ukrainian Miner Rescued from Underground Explosion*

Only the eyes say *human*, the trunk and arms
speechless with animality, immured
in their caked hide, the head a clay melon
sprouting furry leafage. The eyes' thick lids
speak a familiar language of exhaustion;
and we can read the panic flaring from
the bloodshot whites, their anguish at the snarl
that has escaped from the ranged teeth where lips
once smiled, because our greed created this
slide into bestiality. Our will-
to-power carved his subterranean lair
and drove him down the scale of evolution
into a rubble-filled labyrinth where
the monster and the sacrifice are one.

Baucis and Philemon on the No. 5 Bus

They have invited each other in and out
of their bodies and minds for so long the edge of
   mine and *yours* has rubbed away, worn doorsill that
now lets light spill freely through, welcoming morning's
   tides into the dark house, tilting a basin
onto the porch of night.
                      If Jove and Mercury
   took the No. 5 and sat where I do now —
looking down godlike from the raised seats at the back —
   these matching heads of silver might remind them
of another gentle couple nearing eighty
   who alone, in a neighbourhood of barred doors,
unbolted and welcomed the weary disguised gods.
   Baucis and Philemon, each to the other
master and servant, fetched down the precious bacon
   from pumiced rafters, stirred and fed the embers
under their copper pot, trued the leaning table
   with a smoothed shard — all the while keeping their jug
of small talk flowing, in a braid of words and steps
   that captivated the highborn guests.

Yet, though
Jove and his son would have been touched by this couple's
   interlocked hands, their skin's fine rivered parchment,
not even godly eyes can reach beneath lines of
   touch to that inner city where he and she
scale the bone stairways of one another's courtyards
   and share the wine that fountains in one rhythm
through branching, interwoven passageways.
                                                    The gods
   divined such unseen harmonies in their hosts,
sparing the hillside cottage from flood, turning it
   to a marble temple, turning the couple —
once the frail timbers of their bodies began to
   give way — into trees so closely grown
their limbs seemed branches of one rooted trunk.
                                                    I can
   not believe that a marble temple waits to
echo these feet stepping down from the bus, but hope

   their footfalls leaving this world someday will be
so soft because they've cast aside so many of

the thick coverings the soul hides behind.

                                                          If
I haven't followed, the bus window might offer
   me something of their spirit in that little
two-step the light does with the silver maple leaves.

Heroes

1.

Homer's Hector is starting to lose it, ducking
hardware that trims the Mohawk fringe from his helmet,
falling on used-up Trojans littering the beach,

when the last mad Greek he wants to meet, Achilles,
pops up like Death from a toaster. But it's no sweat:
Hector's fairy godfather, Phoebus, pulls the old

cloud trick. Three times the bronze fang lunges at
$\qquad$ Hector,
who thins to zip three times before proud Achilles
sees he's been took.
$\qquad$ Or take Aeneas, collapsing

into his tent, spurting like a leaky wineskin
until godmother Venus spikes the IV drip
with Hero-Aid. He rises shining, blows kisses

to his son, goes forth to make more local orphans.
Each hero back then had his claque, every epic
its balconies crowded with divine cheerleaders.

2.

Alone and unapplauded, Manuel has balanced
between clouds all day. His shirt, a darker blue now
than the sky, clings like a hot wet compress. No god

will peel it from his shoulders and lift him into
the stars. He will climb down the ladder on his own
two feet and, with no waxen wings to melt, survive

to face the ladder tomorrow with another
load of asphalt shingles.
                              In the depths beneath him,
Derek has seen no daylight, smelled no earth, felt no

breeze but the trains of metal-scented wind that roar
through his station before and after the people-
laden trains. The busker who flutes a Coke jingle

across the turnstile will never try to open
his glass cage and pipe him up to the light, away
from his token realm.
                              One level up, the Super

Saver does not stock and will not special order

miraculous rescues, but deals in magic. Chains
no eye can see bind Nadia to the humming

hard-shelled monster whose gliding lower jaw takes in
cash and the hours of her life. No one sees the spear
that stabs the base of her spine, or the stones pressing

all feeling from her feet.
                                      How kind the gods are, in
their neglect, to have let work usurp their place. Now,
where once they melted mortals into streams, work paints

blue rivers on the backs of legs, draws eyes deeper
beneath the ledges it has carved in foreheads, bends
straight bones into arcs and twists. Our heroes are work's

living works of art, no longer silenced to stone,
their words no longer lost in birdsong. They could speak
of the pain if their heroic pride would let them.

The Original Human Blockhead

*Mr. Burkhart, who lived in Riverview, Fla., was one of the last of
the old-time sideshow performers clustered around the Tampa area.*
                        — New York Times, 10 Dec 2001

The big top's folded and they've all gone south
   with Yorick for the long winter —
Revolvo's head won't swivel any more
   to face us over his shoulder blades
and bum, the cheeks of Chimpa the Monkey Girl
   no longer need a trim, and time
has eaten the cotton-candy frizz off Dinah
   the Albina. The ranks of freaks,
both born and made, thin out with all the billowing
   flesh that sailed on Tom Ton's bones.

Melvin, the Original Human Blockhead,
   joins them by choice ("I never have died
before, I'm kinda curious about that")
   at ninety-four, the way at five
he made his body over into a freak show,
   raising the curtain of his shirt
on tumbling stomach muscles, arching his tongue
   to kiss his nose, miming goodbye

with ears wagged in duet. Class show-off, tying
his hands in knots to make theirs clap —

but hardly original. To win wide applause
it took him — would-be boxer, KO'd
six times — a run of losses: consciousness,
blood, teeth, and in his last bout, all
the small bones of his sinuses, prised out
by surgeons, leaving him a cave
to fill most famously. "Anyone who
has ever hammered a nail into
his nose owes a large debt to Melvin Burkhart,"
eulogized one of his protégés.

A sideshow Hamlet unafraid of his
own hollow skull, he held it up
and, Yorick-like, played tricks, riddling its halls
with pointed jokes, drumming music
that echoed off its ivory walls. Homeless
through sixty years of tent-life on
the road, he made himself at home with our
final address, draping the round

sarcophagus with streamers, filling it
   with a calliope's high-pitched hoots.

Master of emptiness, trapeze artist swinging
   on vacancy, tightrope walker
who spurned a wire: since air was his empire,
   and since he never went onstage
without an original sequined fez, I string
   these words — the tongue's glitter — along
an insubstantial thread of breath, weaving
   this crown for his, making an art
of loss to set air ringing while time
   makes freaks and boneheads of us all.

Transformations

Northern portrait masks are carved and painted asymmetrically: the transformation is subtly revealed as the mask is slowly rotated from the head-on view to profile. Other transformation masks consist of an external mask that can be split open to reveal a different form inside.
                                    — from Spirit Faces, by Gary Wyatt

1. Hatchling

When you change from your human shell
to slip into killer whale, shark, coho,
    slow rotation won't do.

The alabaster rigging of
your lungs, where air is spirited to life,
    will flood and go under

before the hull outfits itself
with rows of gills, red-blooded galley slaves
    pumping through cold salt waves.

Better to split. Rip off the pale
tissue paper of skin, cut through rough surf
    in your steel-sequined suit,

and lift as if water were air,
arm winged into pectoral, feet a foam-
slapping scarf of tail fin.

2. Cycling

Green boy on green bike. Slow fade. First
Dad's arm, keeping both afloat, dissolves
    from view. Next, training wheels

zero out. Chain guard exits. Green
fenders slip under black lacquer, then flee,
    spirited off like leaves

or baby fat from the barbed chin
of the spandex-flanked cyclist emerging
    profiled over the flung

water-scarf his bike's skidding wheels
unfurl as they rudder the puddled streets.
    His spiked hair's dorsal fin

splits the damp air yellow zigzag-
ging goggles target through fog. Steel-scaled, an
    earlobe flashes rainbows.

Orpheus Appropriated*

It was one of those mornings when Orpheus,
who'd been torn apart by the loss of Eurydice
    and then again by the winos at Hebrus
was feeling really put together. He needed

    no lyre, humming his latest take
down the steps to the Summerhill subway station.
    But what was that hissing he heard? The snake
who took off his old muse? No, just a take-off

    by a spaced-out imitator's country-and-western
downbeat in a hailstorm of alliteration
    that almost took him out — a close one,
and worse, those rhymes tightening like lariats

    he only just sidestepped. Grateful
as he felt to be remembered after all
    the dismemberment, he wished such yokels
didn't have him at their guitar strings' plucking call.

*Orphism: a mystic Greek religion supposedly founded by Orpheus,
offering release from the cycle of reincarnation. Anakoluthon: lack of
sequence; literally, "not following."

He was sick of being kicked around
from one musical setting to another, black
    and blue from bouncing through the underground
of every no-talent jerk on the Nashville network.

He wanted simply to sink into pallid
obscurity. Had they no pity for his discomposure,
    always the burden of some ballad,
hauled up from rest like an exhumed corpse?

But now, sheer inspiration powered
his train of thought to the line's final station:
    Orphism, forever childless brainchild,
to be nursed by his new Greek girlfriend, Anna
                            Koluthon.

Home Groan

Keats and his inmates heard it
when their ship, driving through the waves off Naples,
    stalled in quarantine, and he
made "more puns, in a sort of desperation,
    in one week, than in any
year of my life." Groans met his fevered efforts
    to work words free from the grip
of fact. Confined to a narrow wooden bunk
    only one side short of a
perfect coffin, he hacked out breathing room, built
    jokey temples where divine
mind lorded over the matter closing in.

This roadside sign has called up
so many groans they hover around it, from
    its Maple Hill Farms title
and its flaking Holsteins, up the lane to, yes,
    a mapled hill, with farmhouse
shaded by trees, barn, silo. The sign's motto
    escapes the black and white of
caption and herd, proclaiming in red Gothic:
    "We love each udder." Like Keats,

Joe Schaap the dairy farmer — though never one
    to own up to a love of
words or love — told out his heart in pun's dumb show.

    Joe's neighbours share the habit.
The poultry farm sells Eggceptional Grade A's
    and, past the bridge, a Seven-
Eleven's donuts go for Holesale Prices.
    Down-home puns, on the border
of poetry — but careful never to stray
    across it, through the dense woods
to fields where sinkholes riddle the solid ground.
    Rather than try to wing it
with full-throated ease, better to groan at mock
    failure, for fear the real thing
will pull you in and close up your mouth with earth.

    Failure's theme song, groans shudder
from Keats's rust-eaten lungs or from any
    body's doomed struggle to keep
up. Uhhh. Yet, in the diaphragm, relief that
    the pun hasn't succeeded

in setting words free from the cage of matter
   takes a deep breath. We fear dis-
embodied words, sound hovering after lips'
   exit, now the name of no
body. The groan fills up the emptiness of
   a Grecian urn, takes the place
of loss. Adam's apple. Adam's atoms. Uhhh.

Petit Ballet

I flip the switch on, and the tiny mice who live
   backstage in my computer tiptoe into
position. You can hear a sleek rustling as they
   fluff their tutus and give the long pink ribbons
of their slippers one last tweak before curtain time.

Choreographer and stage manager, I sit
   in a solitary chair several stories
above the stage. When the footlights come on, they start
   their performances, lining up in response
to the cues I send by tapping on my keyboard.

Quick studies all, all gifted with four nimble feet,
   they translate my finger strokes into *jeter*
and *élever*, holding fixed positions whole hours
   without a wobble. Sometimes I surprise them,
calling for routines they haven't rehearsed in months,

but no sooner do I send the silent command
   to *open* than — the houselights briefly dimming
and flaring — they appear, minute as bands marching
   in formation on some great stadium field,
all perfectly posed, not a looped tail out of place.

Adept at the classical repertoire, which calls
   for massive groupings pressing forward in tight,
mathematically precise configurations,
   they are equally at home with the abstract,
random athletics of contemporary style.

They are also very discreet. Once in a while
   I catch fierce whispers of offstage quarrelling —
perhaps over who gets to play the lead — but these
   turbulent little altercations dissolve
like distant fireworks well before they come onstage.

I've grown increasingly partial to them, impressed
   by their professionalism — a contrast
to the behaviour of foreign troupes who tumble
   (jet-lagged?) from the wings for guest appearances
in helter-skelter gyrations that make no sense.

My one worry is how this corps sustains itself.
   No one sends out for food — no period-sized
pizzas, no grocery.com deliveries —
   and when I leave bites of cheese temptingly near
the backstage door, I find them dry and unnibbled.

Yet maybe this reticence also stems from their
     discretion. After all, I see them only
a small part of each day, mostly during evening
     performances; like theirs, my work patterns are
nocturnal. Who knows what feasts, what orgies they throw

when I'm away. I think I may even have seen
     the inky dots of their eyes peeking out from
the CD slot, checking whether those paws that prowl
     the keyboard have moved off, tied up in some game
dragging a yellow stick across a bare white stage.

The Figure a Poem Makes

Like a piece of ice on a hot stove the poem must ride on its own melting.
— *Robert Frost*

Cold comfort from Frosty the Snowman.
Perhaps it worked for him, his hangouts
and hang-ups more boreal. Walking
in the frozen swamp on an old man's
winter night, watching his woods fill up
with snow, he had half a chance to get
the ice cube to the stove unmelted.

My poetics trickle down to me
not from Frosty, but from a warmer,
more domestic seasonal icon,
the Easter Bunny: one specific
chocolate Easter Bunny who lives
in the April woods of lost childhood.

I left him on the windowsill, pure
sweet promise, untouched except in my
hungry imagination. When I
returned from church, the afternoon sun
had transubstantiated him to varnish.

Since then, I haven't trusted Frosty's
figures and haven't believed the ads:
there will *always* be chocolate mess
with M&Ms, with Ps, Ts, any
letters. The taste the melted vision
leaves on the page will never equal
what never met the tongue. I'll always
be left licking my sticky fingers,
waiting for next year's resurrection.

End of the Line

infini-
>   and the thirsty eye, reaching for the t
>   of infinity, lands in the desert of
tesimal.

Bad break, making riches
>   to rags look less like
>   dip than blip.

Nosebleed-breeding dive,
>   an allornothing plunge from
>   pinnacle to abyss.

This pocketsize apocalypse,
>   cameo catastrophe,
swings on an all-embracing i,
>   then drops to near-zero,

>   broken, a tragic hero
>   sheared of eternal life in a mere
hyphen.

Handwriting on the Wall[*]

Sometimes art tells life's future, but life —
too dumb to understand, too deep in now
   to rise to then — goes on ogling its
new Rolex during the last step before
   air tries and fails to take the place of
cliff, or it lets the cell phone's windblown surf
   drown out the avalanche's whispers.

"Hey Belshazzar," some sober guest cries
as the host rises to toast himself, "look
   behind you." Too late, and anyway
the Hebrew anagram's too hard for these
   meshugge gentiles to crack. Yet, such
graffiti doesn't flow only from the
   gold magic marker of God's finger.

*Domenico Fetti's "David with the Head of Goliath" and Cristofano Allori's "Judith with the Head of Holofernes" were acquired by King Charles I between 1625 and 1627 and are part of the Royal Collection in London. Van Dyke's portrait of Charles I and Rembrandt's "Belshazzar's Feast," both painted 1637-1638, hang in the National Gallery. Overthrown by Cromwell's Parliamentary forces in the English Civil War, Charles was executed by them in 1649.

Sometimes it comes from a poet's pen,
as when Shelley's wrote "A restless impulse
    urged him to embark and meet lone Death
on the drear ocean's waste," years before a
    restless impulse urged him to embark
and meet lone Death on the drear ocean's waste.
    And sometimes the writing on the wall

    can be a picture: Charlie Chaplin's
toothbrush-moustached face, hugely moonlit on
    thousands of cinema walls. Decades
later the imp, turning vicious, sprouted
    fangs beneath the bristles, ironed a
swastika over the heart on his sleeve
    and goose-stepped his way over Europe.

    Or these two pictures King Charles the First
bought for his Royal Collection. If you
    listen, you can hear the parting shot
David slings at Charles from Fetti's canvas:
    "Yo! Dude!" — running fingers through the fur
of Goliath's lopped-off head — "Dream on, if
    you think riding some giant horse will

save your neck from what I did to his.
Higher-ups make great targets for squirts
   who can't afford not to fight dirty.
I could take *you* out at twice the distance!"
   The other picture's silent, Judith
not one to crease the satin of her brow
   with an emotion. Nonchalantly

   she holds — well out from the gold brocade —
her trophy, and in its tormented face
   (said to be Allori's self-portrait)
Charles might have read his horoscope: "Bridle
   rising expectations. Underlings'
plans should be carefully scrutinized for
   private agendas. Keep a cool head."

   But Charles's head is still in the clouds,
a noble bust in the equestrian
   portrait he commissioned from Van Dyke
to look down on the Davids and Judiths.
   Art draws our stirrup-high eyes up to
his moustached face, caught in the V of a
   Van Dyke beard, propped for the headsman's stroke.

Spaced Out

A terse note from the department chair
has come back with my completed copy
of the Survey on Office Space, which he
declines to forward to the dean's committee.

He rejects my proposal that the Faculty of Medicine
embrace the open concept and quarter its staff
on gurneys stationed at regular intervals
under the fluorescent lights of one long corridor,

questions the wisdom of housing the Division
of Mining and Metallurgy in a maze of interconnected
catacombs running beneath the football stadium
and accessible via low-roofed, cage-doored elevators,

dismisses as fatuous the idea that law students
waiting along mahogany panelling
outside the double doors to the faculty spa
should submit hourly dockets to parking meters,

but reserves his fiercest scorn (with threats
only lightly veiled) for my suggestion
that the Office of the Chair be just that: straight-
                              backed, wooden,
extended on a simple plank from its third floor window.

The Neighbourhood of Words

We breeze right by it in unchronicled
odysseys, launches and returns
from one bay of the house to another.

No wonder. Those upright, shuttered facades
give only marginal glimpses
of the vast otherness burning inside.

Each lodged bookmark, captured in profile, turns
a thin chimney where still thinner
heat-spirits shinny up ropes of pure light.

Through one low arch, under burrowed ceilings,
the eye of a volcano flares
from a white-bearded wizard's blown smoke rings.

Two women at a tall window look past
time to a lighthouse. One feels its
rays as brushstrokes, one sees them as her pulse.

Behind the oak door, a barge floats on fire.
Two lovers flame and melt in one
another's arms, their love their funeral pyre.

So many neighbours, shut-ins without us.
All of us, without them, huddled
in caves under our own trembling shadows.

This Hunger Lives

in a sodden hut near the two trees of your lungs.
   He never leaves, never eats, keeps himself alive
      with sips from the rusty creek that passes through it.

He lives only for the skin drum he squats over
   day and night. The beat his hands beg from it rises
      above the storm blowing through the two trees'
                        branches

and pulses colours on the white cloud of your mind.
   For he knows how you crave those heavenly pictures,
      how much of life you live ascending into them

in the hours when the world's clouds are lost in darkness.
   He lightens you, drumming up flowers to soften
      footfalls on mountain paths, powdering the flowers

into a shimmer that pillows your steps beyond
   the mountain's peak. Walls, in the houses he wakens,
      doorway at your approach, and from the canvas bag

you carry, the forgotten toys of your childhood
    seek your grip. For he also knows the past is lodged
        deeper than mountains are high, harder to enter

than stone; and knowing this, he loves you so dearly
    he beats his palms raw to draw your dead familiar
        voices up like water in a bucket. Spilling

through the tent flap of your sleeping ear, they gather
    beneath the dome and flood it with tuneless lyrics,
        their thin refrains the echoes of echoes, lacking

a beat. One night, when the drummer's love of music
    calls him in pity to give it, he will rise from
        his hut and carry you with him, past the still trees.

Higher Education

When you first climbed the stepladder
of capital A, your reward
was to have the ladder vanish
into sound holed up in your throat.

So you ate the world, capital
B's butterfly wings fluttering
over your lips, C threading through
windswept passes between your teeth.

Course by course, the alphabet served
its dinner of letters to you,
and your body changed their matter
into the energy of voice.

Then the letters came together
and the process reversed: when A
met X, your energy fused them
into a polished blade that swung

out of your thought and sank its edge
deep in the thick log of the world.

You're beyond that large-print speller
now. Pick up the axe your letters

gave you a handle on, and cleave
the world back into leaf-filled life
by reading it. Swing your keen eyes
clear of the book's hidebound doorway

and slice the hard rind from the O
of objects. Feed on their sweet fruit.
Read *climbing* from a fixed ladder,
blossoming in an orange wing,

and decipher evolution's
course from the curl of a sea wave.
After these practice sessions, turn
to the world's most exalted text.

Read speech as music in the air
where lips return your lips' touch. Read
your self to heaven in a face
where love, with two eyes, draws your I.

Speech Therapy

His love speaks the language of love
more lithely than the sage linguists.
Her lips and teeth negotiate
its iterative straits and twists
as fleet as neon pulsing through
the uncials and cursives of
the night's calligraphy.
                         Her love
speaks volumes with his hands, grasping
the branching, transformational
syntax and deep structure of
a dialect of rounded vowels.

Their love's a love of discourse held
in conversations where, amid
a theory of performance and
a generative grammar all
fricative and labial,
the tongue's licked into shape.

All Day Dim Sum

dim sum, which means touch the heart
— *OED*

On the long bus ride

he and she eat Chinese words

from each other's lips.

Words for Gabrielle at Three Months

1.
Flaked-out, all limbs limp, deep
in what your father calls your Jell-O mode,
you sleep rocked in my cradling arm

doubly covered, under wool
your great-grandmother crocheted for your mother
and under the lighter shawl our restless

maple knits and unravels
with spills of sun. All afternoon, you
and the tree have sung duets for me

in sign language — branch
dip, fist clench, lip pucker, leaf flick. The tree
has given over throat-language

to robins and finches. Your
gift is yet to come, stitchwork of words
shuttling through the loom of breath.

2.
Ever-living fabric,
breath-born words, not to be yielded for
their dried remains laid out on paper —

black magic that Huang Che
stole from bird footprints, hoarding breath better spent
in song, turning wind under wing

to the dead weight of stone.
After he wrote the first words, he wept all night,
well-meaning hit man in the takedown

of soul by body. Breath,
unlike ink, makes poor mortar for building
monuments — won't set, spills

from lips, bears no one's name
for long, slips out so quick on cold mornings
it drops its shadow — yet the humming-

bird of your breath flies from
the flower in your chest and sets mine trembling
as no word written ever will.

3.
Dear heart, if I'm away
when you have words for me, don't put them down
in print. Courier them, folded

in whispers, over waves
of breath warm with the life of all babblers —
you, your messenger, the maple

with its chatter of birds,
the mothers and fathers whose lullabies weave through
those of the winds that cradle them.

If I'm napping, out of
hearing, you'll breathe me awake in your life
and sing me into your words.

III

September Song

Two hands can clap, two legs can dance: among
the comforts of this world under one sun,

these twins that keep each other company.
Two eyes share the sights like a couple on holiday,

the left ear and the right pour out their jugs
together in the brain's vat, and the lungs

divvy up and then give back their catch
of air in harmony. How kind of nature

to deal out pairs. Wise also, to allow
for chance. If one hand suffers a letdown,

the other carries on; when one ear's foyer
shuts, sound still finds an unlocked door.

So, following nature's lead, the architect
framed a duet in glass and concrete. Yet,

nature brought down his artful counterpoint
with a more primitive rhythm, percussive chant

that, caged for life, plucking its bloody strings,
the spiteful heart in solitary sings.

Van Gogh: Thatched Cottages
at Cordeville (1890)

All prey to a tidal wave of green flame, garden
   upon garden, house upon house, the stone
     endwall of the nearest house unable

to dam the churning torrent that will
   overtake it soon as the artist's back
     is turned — he died the year he painted it — when

gyrating emerald fireballs, once
   mere rooted trees, completely overrun
     the thatch they've all but razed at the far end.

Already the houses thicken with darker
   shades of the same grey bursts of ash that nearly
     blot out the sky's blue. Two white-spindled windows

blacken with soot. Already grasses and shrubs
   kindle sympathetically into self-immolating
     undulation. The crooked line of split-

rail fencing closest to us shrivels like spent
    matchsticks, softens to a blur in the infernal
        glow, will never hold against the flood.

And did you think, the artist asks, that straw
    and slat or stone and flesh might ever survive
        this all-consuming tide? That the blade-edge

of a painting's frame could staunch it?

Glastonbury Abbey

*A true building builds you up as you look at it. The pleasures
of . . . ruins are not infinite.*
                                    — *Charles Tomlinson*

But these ruins are. Here you build yourself
a world as airy and unmortared as
the future — one that assembles, stone by
phantom stone, as your eye fills in the blanks

between columns with webs of coloured glass
and rainbows those tall stumps with an arched roof.
Under its beams, the monks you resurrect
file in for vespers, and their massed voices

echo off iron fittings which your mind
forges on recomposed oak altar rails,
while farther back, along more ancient stairs,
Arthur steps down from storied Avalon.

Wells Cathedral, Afloat

Light spreads it maplike on the water's glass-topped table,
  sleeks the seamless join of sky and stone.
    Light's ripples whisper to your soul
      this is the real cathedral.

Where liquid air laps liquid arches that support
  a dove-grey haze of ashlar, buttresses
    flutter their wings and God's house sails,
      both ark and Ararat.

The master mason and his fellows carved a vision:
  these wells its harbour, hooded from Atlantic winds
    by mortared walls that bishops and deans
      put their solid faith in.

Masons knew stone too well to trust their heaven to it.
  Earth-anchored, blind to light, pried from its bed
    with pain, the Judas stone betrayed
      their backs and drank their blood.

They raised that pile as template for this floating prayer.
Here no roof argues with the stars, no tower
shadows the houses of the poor.
The walls are holy water.

Within, the font refills itself and overflows,
flooding the crypt where sun-scaled rainbows spawn.
Rooted tendrils of a true vine
thread the Jesse window.

Knock, and the door will open, softly taking your hand.
To enter, you must give up all you have,
blow your last breath back to land,
let your lips close on heaven.

Cross Road Blues

They live at the cross road, this old couple
some folks know as Mama Soul and Papa Body,
some as Mama Body, Papa Soul.

Live in the same old house, but since they're blind
and forever lose and find each other, the house
plays out wails of the lost, whoops of the found.

This man slides a piece of broken glass
over the long neck, searching for his soul. No blood,
but the long wail that opens Cross Road Blues

pours from the mouth of his guitar. He would
climb into that mouth if he could. Across its bars
slender fingers flutter like a trapped bird.

This other man's fingers fly: when Marcus
Roberts' trio lights into Robert Johnson's
Cross Road, no body's home, a soul's wail soars

over the keys, that single note (muttbone
or vocal, who can tell?) an angel's whirr of wing
unsettling as the moon, homeless in heaven,

a soul as lonely in its uprising
as Johnson on his knees, the man and the angel
singing the blues in solo all night long.

This pair have found each other, Mama Soul's
white feathers flutter as she and Papa Body
sweep across a few feet of celluloid

in nineteen thirty-four: Ginger and Fred
dance cheek to cheek, the charm about her has carried
him through to heaven, his tapping black-shoed

feet and hers (feather-draped) curvet and glide
in frothy syncopated grooving, no cross road
for them but loops right back in curlicued

ravellings that play out the plot's contrived
arrivals and departures, or the art deco'd
setting (some Venice of the wishful mind

floating above the dark brown fascist ground),
an unearthly blue where Fred and Ginger unwind
forever in Hollywood's neverland.

❦

This other pair have held one note, Mary
and Gabriel in consort for five hundred years.
Who can tell which is soul, which body?

The angel on his knees, and Mary (eyes
deeply entranced, half-closed) dance together, their hands
palm-up, fingering the divine on keys

unseen, their steps so smooth they seem to stand
still in the room where Botticelli painted them,
its earth-toned walls broken by the window

through which the angel (robe still puffed with heaven)
just alighted to call her from her music stand
to be the song. No road but a river

unwinds behind them, nothing to suggest
the cross except one figured in a distant tree
and in red folds spilling from her blue dress.

Ten Angels and a Hero

It's 1932. Eleven men
   sit on an I-beam in mid-air
like sparrows wing to wing along a wire.
Death, disguised as nothing, waits to catch them

and snaps this photo to make light of miles
behind their backs. He tricks the whole west side,
   Hudson river, palisades,
to fade like painted tracks into the horizon's

smoke-screened tunnel. Far below, his playful
   thumb and finger have stacked up
a miniature city, block on block
too toy to be the end of a great fall.

Ten of the clutch, immune to Death's teasing,
have left their bodies to their sandwiches
   and hover over the branches
of one another's thoughts. Immortal wings,

with shutter speeds beyond the camera's,
    steep them in heavenly currents
whose perfect buoyancy flows through their shirts
and rises as mist from their distant gazes.

The lone eleventh workman holds a drained,
flask-shaped bottle and looks at us. Eyes great
    with nothing know that if he drops it
it will fall and fall, and the angels won't hear a sound.

Touch[*]

1.

The swoosh behind me means Fra Sebastiano's here.

In an age of tall belief — when angel wings winked
like traffic lights from every corner, when fountains
turned pink from water's leaps into wine, and surges
of resurrection broke through snow-shrouded pavement
all winter long — a rustle of silk would unfurl
some divine annunciation.

        But he swoops in
grumbling — no harp, no trumpet. And no angel's feet
blacken the carpet like those size fourteens as he
fidgets, settling his threadbare robe on my sofa.
He's never even seen an angel, except in
paintings.

        Paintings, it turns out, bring him here tonight
with all his foul-breathed bellyaching. (I've often

---

[*] According to the Gospel of St. John (20:14-18), the risen Christ appears as
a gardener to Mary Magdalene. When she gestures to him, he replies *Noli me
tangere* (Touch me not). In the 1440s, Fra Angelico painted frescoes of this and
other Biblical incidents for the cells of the monastery of San Marco in Florence.
My fictional Fra Sebastiano, as supervisor of the lay brothers, would have lived
in the cell where *Noli me tangere* is depicted.

told him his visits would be so much easier
to take if he didn't starve himself — how sinful
can bedtime snacks be? — but he calls that blaspheming
and keeps his reeking fasts.) And keeps on ranting now
about two frescoes, the one of Christ in Limbo
next door in Brother Alfonso's cell, the other
on his own wall.

        Green devils, crouched in the corners
of limbo, give young Alfonso nightmares. He wakes
with screams that would rouse the whole dormitory if
Fra Sebastiano didn't dash in to calm him,
hush with soothing words, hand smoothing the damp
                                 forehead
"the way my mother did if I woke feverish,
sixty years ago, long before Angelico
called up sights that cast fevers on the heart.
                     The boy
calls me his saviour, reaches out like Abraham
welcoming Our Lord in the fresco. I make light
to cheer him, say oh but my coming didn't sweep
the door from its hinges or flatten a horned fiend
underneath."

He sighs. "Then I go back to my cell,
and my own fresco visits a nightmare on me
while I sit wide awake watching the soft fingers
of first light work the stuccoed corners around it
into shape. Light, God's first creation, delivers
me and my room from the black-draped, windowless house
of night, calling even the tiniest dust motes
to rise up and dance. It reaches the panel last,
on the wall beside the casement.

                              There the nightmare
grips me, because that fresco — which could never speak
but for the touch of light — comes alive and glowers
'Don't Touch!' Mary Magdalene, kneeling, stretching out
hands to embrace Our resurrected Lord, meets with
an arm's-length warding-off. His hands are out of bounds,
and His feet — once bathed with her tears, wiped with
                                     her hair —
float above the ground like water lilies as they
sashay away."

                    I break the silence he lets fall:
"Where's the nightmare? Isn't that what your religion
says resurrection's all about? Single-minded

as the boulder rebounding from his tomb, new life
rises and tells the old life to kiss off."

                                 "No stone,"
he thunders, "more solid than your unbelieving
head! How can I give it eyes?"

                                Then, more calmly: "God
forgive my impatience. Let me try to explain.
If Our Lord spurns even the loving hand, is all
we touch, and all that touches us, to be cast off
as impure? A voice, a painting, that seems to reach
into our soul? Light itself? — Are these no more than
so many green devils? What on earth is the use
of everything on earth?"

                              With each question, he grew
fainter, then faded out altogether in a
negative incarnation, the spirit of doubt
filling, replacing, the body it had possessed.

2.

Another night, some nights later. Another swoosh,
this one impassioned, the skirt of his robe slapped down
beside him — smack of a judge who brings his court to
order, the verdict reached: "The hoe proves it!"

        "The hoe?"
"And to think I looked at it all these years without
seeing, without even asking why Our Saviour,
new-risen, would be shouldering a hoe. A glimpse
of Alfonso at work in the cloister garden
sent me running upstairs to compare his real hoe
with the painted one. Useless in the tomb Jesus
came from, useless in the heaven he was bound for,
but — obvious now — useless in any garden,
the blade so thin you can see the tree behind it
through it!"
      "The artist's mistake," I suggested.
                "No,
the beholder's mistake, for taking as a tool
the sign Angelico left — his sharp hint about
touching. *Noli me tangere* doesn't mean touch
is forbidden, it means it's been made as useless
as a hoe of air. Mary doesn't need to touch
in order to reach the risen Christ who's with her,
through her, the way light infuses that hoe. To touch,
to be touched: what are these but groping to make one
of two, to dissolve what separates?"
          "Not so fast.

That may have worked for Christ and Mary Magdalene,
but you still haven't answered your own nightmare: what's
the use of all those things we do touch?"

"The hoe gleams
with insight here again. Its transparency stands
for the essential lightness of what we reach for
when we reach out to things. The hand grasps at a scrap
of bread not to hold it but to feel the release
of a hold that grips our insides. The dry tongue seeks
freshness and coolness in the guise of water. Eyes —
look at the fresco of St. Dominic looking
up at Our Lord's face on the cross — search other eyes
seeking infinities of love. The most dense stone" —
and here he focussed on my forehead with a smile
even he would call devilish — "is doorway to
mystery, and matter the picture of spirit.
As you might write, in the poem you'll make of this
when I've gone back to 1482, we keep
in touch" — he faded — "to put ourselves out of touch."

Touch Is

embraced as legal

tender in the counting house

of the human heart.

David Gazes at Bathsheba's Foot-Washing

You can understand why
for some eyes, feet
detonate the ultimate
orgasmic explosion.

Kept, like denizens
of a harem, from sight,
white and protected,
they have mystique.

Lacking the muscled
deftness of hands,
they are plump little birds
twittering their toes.

When touched, they arch
the way whole bodies
do when doing
naughty things.

Totally disarmed,
the toes hug each other,
powerless against
a feather's tickle.

Humble, abashed:
when the rest of the body
rises and stretches
they kiss the floor.

You can understand why —
for men who like
their women quiet,
pliant and deferent —

down there with feet,
which everybody
walks all over,
is where it's at.

Vermeer: Towards *The Concert*

She knew his need to re-invent the room
each time, as if the chair, the tapestry
that draped the table — even her own dress —
were notes on parchment that he strained to read,
holding this way then that against the light
until they yielded up gems of music.

The last thing on his mind now was music.
Dragging oak and brocade around the room
to catch light thirsted after as if light
were water and they the rucked tapestry's
tropical growth, he studied how she read:
the centred book, composure of the dress.

Helpless, she'd watched him shock the yellow dress
to ghostliness, upsetting The Music
Lesson by stepping in before he'd read
fault lines that fractured his scaled, sidelit room
and stranded her. The skulking tapestry
crouched at the rift and lapped up her warm light.

So he'd begun again, grounding the light
in a gold arc that surged along her dress

from window frame to jug to tapestry,
her outstretched hands conducting a music
heard with the eye in close-up, with no room
for light to be mislaid or notes misread.

Then came the painting where, hand poised, she read
a balance weighted with small pearls of light,
herself a balance, bearing up the room's
dark freight with the new life her bell-shaped dress
billowed around, sounding blue veiled music
to charm the shadow from the tapestry.

Now he approached the chair, the tapestry,
her face, her thoughts, as shadows to be read
rather than gems to hold. He saw music
echoed the pitched elusiveness of light,
worn for a brief space as the spirit's dress,
but barred to entry, like a painted room.

Or a real tapestry. So Vermeer read
that third into the room: singer, blue-dressed,
whose raised hand's music marries theirs with light.

Homing

The Holy Land is no special place. It is every place that has ever been recognized and mythologized by any people as home.
                                        — *Joseph Campbell*

A keyturn banks your engine's
    furnace for the evening.
        You and a few friends, shedding

vehicles bound by earthly
    limits at curbside, drape
        outerwear over the coat rack,

take up stations around
    the board, start to let slip
        the shadowy veils of substance.

Each of you picks a simple
    token in a primary colour
        to bear the soul's weight.

Your host's closed fist
    inverts to cobra head:
        from its rattling mouth

spill the cubed and numbered
  bones, foretelling steps,
    dividing your path by turns.

Outside, a rising moon
  breaches the dam of night
    and pours down water

so thin and otherworldly
  it seeps through windowglass
    to float your tokens along

the dry, buoyant board.
  More liquid ice than water,
    coldness of a light

wrung from shadow, it drains
  everything it floods —
    glow from the tokens, grip

from hands that touch them,
  gravity from minds
    that move the hands. Free

of the pull of earth's iron core,
  you lift remembered glimpses
    of rockfaces and forests

to landscape the game's bare spaces.
  Tree roots slide from their ground
    like untied threads, reweaving

through newly landed carpets
  of moss. The drifting, opaque
    clouds of boulders roll

into hollows, or heap up across
  moonsilvered streams between spaces.
    Breathing no air now

but the game, each of you makes
  winning or losing moves.
    Some players spiral, caught

in plumes of thought, some plunge
  when broken concentration
    collapses a stone bridge.

All will be rescued,
     not just one who reaches
          the goal and sits at the centre,

in the game's final moment,
     a rehearsal for the evening
          when the sky's furnace is banked

for good. So, now, obeying
     your wishful heart, you call
          the end of the game *home*.

Prehistory Revisited

Who can eat from an empty pot? What can you find
but hunger in the hollow of a skull? Once soft
tissue has tiptoed from the scene, poor bones lose touch,
lacking lips to kiss, forgetting their mother tongues.
Question them all day and they will never answer.

My New School of Enlightened Archaeology
won't offer Elementary Fossil-Hunting
or Advanced Endoskeletal Reconstruction,
nor will you learn in a master class to raise pots
from shards with a wizard-like wave of your glue stick.

On your first field trip you'll sit crosslegged, linking
                                                    hands
with the others around a yellowed skeleton
and think its epidermis layer by layer
back over bared sticks and knobs. The loom of your
                                                    thoughts
will clothe bone in a body stocking of feeling.

Then you will all meditate on the weight of time
until the sky overhead turns lead and presses
you down to microscopic smallness and lightness.
Humble as dust, still holding hands, your circle will
float like the outline of a pill past giant lips

down the pink shaft, to land in a chalk-columned hall
under the heart's chandelier — cold crystal before
your footfalls awaken the rainbow-painted moths
of remembrance lodged in its sockets, and their wings
hum the lost beat to life. Now, dancing to its tune,

you will learn more than a thousand Rosetta stones
could tell you about your brothers and sisters from
the past. You will decipher glances that compressed
vast data banks of experience in a wink,
and follow trackless steps of breath as — cloaked only

in a filmy weave of speech — it navigated
chasms between isolated bodies. Hopping
a synapse to the cells of a honeycombed cave,
you'll tour where the duller hominoids learned to bore
with clumsy tools enshrined in modern museums,

while their quick-witted friends picked up
painting, chanting, storytelling. You will ride home
on the slipstream of a shaman's premonition
of your fame for having unearthed the Stone Age's
true name: the Age that Dreamt All the Other Ages.

Commuter Shamans, 7 a.m.

Past the end of the open platform
the black mouth waits — flickering silver
tongue not yet hissing
through the downpour.

Shamans fresh from one more spell
of patient fasting in their dark
study of death's posture
stand huddled

on the platform, each canopied
by a small dome of night that glitters
where rain stars the black gauze.
Their bodies

are bound for cover thicker than
this November morning lowers
over them, but not deeper
than sleep's tunnels.

When the piped chimes sound and doors
slide shut, the shamans reach inside

to free the red bird for
   its spirit journey.

One, whose steel-toed shoes will hold
a ladder's tread all day while thick-gloved
   hands splice and fasten,
      feels the loose sand's

waves slide under bared dreamfeet.
Another climbs a rockface, page
   by page. She rounds the ridge
      and pivots

onto a summit whose distant ever-
green forests, river-mirrored, will
   window the blank wall
      of her office.

This one sees longed-for eyes staring
from a strange face across the aisle.
   The power of her desire
      to stroke his hair

turns its grey stubble to a spring pasture.
In less than the stretch from Summerhill
    to Rosedale, all the hearts
        have flown so far

wet floors and dripping umbrellas
melt into legend. Mists fragrant
    with train-spoor lift and disperse
        from sunswept rails.

IV

Canoe Lake

He took advantage of the leeching effect of the wood on the medium. . . . He painted to the loss of oil which gave, despite the swift brushing, a firmness plus weight and texture to pigment.
— Harold Town, on Tom Thomson

1.
Yr. obedient servant,
   it signs on the iron Shield,
      prostrate under the glower

of an August sky. Will take
   any shape the stone-lipped shore
      dictates, grimace but gather

pebbles thrown at it, offer
   its unblemished skin as a
      mirror for you to admire

yours in. Sidles up — *kiss me,*
   sip me — with the lisp of a
      precocious cousin. Gives back

your own blue gaze, reminds you
　　your body's also mostly
　　　water.
　　　　　　Don't be taken in:

when its sister Night comes home
　and darker waves flood the sky,
　　it will show its colours, turn

snarling at the merest breath
　of wind, curling its lips of
　　ink, flashing white fangs.

2.

He got the proportions right.
  Upper three-quarters unin-
    habitable sky, two-thirds

of what's left unbreathable
  water, land a strip of pelt
    floating between. Step into

a canoe, as he did, you'll
  feel how the human teeters
    thinly. No canoe, the lake's

here for keeps, will be blushing
  like this at sunrise hundreds
    of years after the pelt's been

stripped from you. He reads the *no*
  in Canoe Lake, lifts (as in
    portage) your gaze over land

to the more than skin-deep shore
  he paints high up: two headlands
    of sand-pale cloud from the east

knit with two inlets of sea-
   blue sky from the west, as if
      the water and earth that lie

below were his easel's lip
   merely supporting the real
      scene, the dreamt one you sail on

3.

with no risk of drowning like
    him.
            Yet you will, someday, go
        under water or earth. Light

from a painted sky's too thin
    to float your canoe through night,
        the lake's big sister. Yours too —

always giving you lessons
    in falling, pulling covers
        over your dreams to warm them

and the misty ones the lake
    breathes from its sleep in the bed
        beside yours. Under the high

roofbeams you learn lake water's
    not your cousin but your twin —
        why else would he have painted

waves coursing pink with the same
  lifeblood, thinned down to speed it
    through aeons? — nowhere more twin

than in its black moods, never
  happy in one position,
    reaching to take the shape of

dreams.
        Yet capable of calm
  you might follow, as when he,
    sensing in its rest the lake's

answer to the leeching earth,
  paid firm homage with his brush.
    Let water's calm fill your breast

to give the heart smooth passage
  come the day to launch it, as
    he did, from this strip of coast.

Bows & Arrows*

1.

His hand calls up the dance, his rainbow sticks
lay down the strokes of moccasins circling,

beating the prairie's tanned drumskin, rethread
bright life ribboning the rawhide capes: red-

breasted swallows, blue-plumed dragonflies whose
darts and plunges outwing unfledged arrows

fired from army carbines. Sometimes. Or if
not he can hold the crumpling warhorse in

the air, head and neck looped like a snail shell
under the forelegs back up towards the tail,

hold as in a quiver arrowing spray
from bridled mouth and flanks before it spreads

*Yellow Nose, warrior leader of the Cheyenne, created extraordinary ledger
book drawings of the Plains people's Ghost Dance and of their battles with
the American cavalry in the 1870s. Today, as a result of nuclear testing and
nuclear waste, much Plains land has become toxic — a word whose Ancient
Greek root, τοξα, means "bows" or "arrows."

a scarlet blanket on the dust. He frees
the headlong falling chief's hand from the reins

to count coup on the falling sun. He draws
a yellow-arrowed crown for them to share.

2.

But here if his hand moved it could not stop
arrows the nuclear storm's rainbow shot

into the bones of children playing in
the fine grey snow, into cattle browsing

irradiated forage that windlike
carried the contamination through milk

down the children's throats to where the poisoned
tips of all the arrows in breath or blood

counted coup. His hand, thwarted from tracing
invisible weapons, would find no use

for coloured pencils where no meadowlark
unfolds its yellow vest, no teal flings back

an underwing's green gleam, and no purple
lizard seeks rock ledges blown to powder

when colourless men struck the horizon
and turned seed-bearing earth to ground barren

as the white bow drawn in the night's black sand.

Untrees

From gravel patches and cracked asphalt
under the raised roadbed rise untrees.

Branchless, leafless, they take nothing from
the earth, give back nothing to the air.

Soot, not moss, mounts bark-bare trunks, winter-
rigid through all seasons, heartwoodless

pillars. Their cathedral lacks windows
or walls, the altar they lead to fumes

in unblessed distance. No choir loft hangs
from the vaulted roof they support, though

metal birds wheel above it, too un-
resting to nest. Whose songs bruise heaven.

Psalm

— from the German of Paul Celan

Nobody kneads us again from earth and clay,
nobody hallows our pollen.
Nobody.

Praise be to thee, Nobody.
For thy sake will
we flower.
Towards
Thee.

A nothing
were we, are we, shall
we be, flowering:
the Nothing's, the
Nobody's rose.

With
soul-bright pistil,
heaven-ravaged pollen,
crown red
with the crimson word we sang
evermore over
the thorn.

Torch Singer

In the forest, long
after its tables
of sunlight have been
cleared, after the small
cricket ensembles
have packed up and left
and rows of cushioned
toadstools sit empty,
she comes in, the old
woman who washes
the floor and sings what
you know are the blues
because her low notes
coat the pine needles
with indigo and
the lyrics matter
less than the cloudy
refrains of sorrow
that sweep across but
never stifle this
torch song, of love so
long unrequited

she has become the
torch she holds, a stone-
faced, dry-eyed, bald but
white-hot soprano.

Words & Wings

1.

Bright mouths pour out fresh
passion. Words, worm-riddled, smudge
   the wet lips with dust.
Is *I love you* young or old?

   Crack the wrinkled shell
of a walnut open. Are
   those cloistered leaf-shapes
halves of a brown heart, or wings?

2.

   The green, succulent
flesh of a walnut tree's fruit
   falls away to earth
from the bone-brittle shell. That

   panelled coach rides out
summer storms, falls, cracks open
   on this pair. Call them
Romeo and Juliet,

   two sets of wings in
embrace, shoulders kept apart

by a thin par-
tition of brown film, the pair

wed below the waist.
Not penetration: deeper,
conjoined like the four
chambers of a single heart,

so single-minded
as they beat out the rhythm
of their pure passion.
May some god hear the old young

prayer these make in their
embrace, grant them power to
rise beyond time, lithe
as newly winged butterflies.

Or if not to fly,
to age into a tree, wings —
call them Unfurl and
Spread — bound only by the sky.

What the Tree Knows

1. Optics

Empty sockets deface your trunk.
The white stick of your taproot nods

through thicker darkness than we know
in our day-broken nights.
                              Yet, you

are the long-lived amphibian,
burrower of both earth and sky.

April brings your brown forehead more
green eyes than a thousand seers,

awake at dawn, taking it in.
Needing no go-betweens of brush

or pigment, your enlightened art
teaches insight how to blossom.

2. Ethics

Since you can make the bitter clay
run clear and sweet inside you, do

we owe all our sweetness to those
plums and peaches we have swallowed?

Can you yield enough to freshen
the earth we soil and feed the life

we blight?
   Though we will never know
the good of purifying air

simply by breathing out, your fixed
stance can teach us patient waiting

for the right wind.
    We can learn to
praise it with raised and waving limbs.

3. Metaphysics

If a breath stops in the city,
you sense it as if another

tree fell in the forest, reading
beyond our ken an alphabet

of ether.
        The clock face you know
does not retrace a track, but grows

outwards in rings: you intuit
life's essential rounds not buried

in dead wood, but running closest
to the life around them.
                Your deaths —

falls of leaf, fungus-ledge, sunlight
to forest floor — rise as that life.

Spring Returns

Especially on a day when wind and snow
knot the pink wings of newly hatched magnolia
in a white frieze, you search for spring. Find it. Go
back up the long, wooden-stepped escalators
of the old Eaton's department store which no
longer exists, up to the drapery floor
like hummingbirds or bees who find the sun's glow
on grey days in the tasselled suns of flowers.

Flip through thick books of samples. Choose the yellow
sheer that gave lift to icebound casements
all the long winter in your first apartment.

Hover floorless there. You won't fall. If salmon
petalled with silver can soar back, you must know
the gills in your chest will thread sun through your veins.

Tidings

On the other side of this wall our old mother's hands
  (mantilla of wrinkles afloat on the silk-thin skin)
    rehearse the deaf composer's unfinished sonata.

Like everything else in her world, the keyboard meanders:
  tremors carried up and down its ivories shift it
    over the sand-burnished inlays of her clean-swept floor.

She meanders, memory a school of fish lost in
  depths the sun never reaches, where no landmark
                                                    endures
    the current that erodes a moment's features

blank. For countless moments you swam in her womb,
                                              your fist
  closing on nothing till birth opened years of minutes
    for lungs to breathe and your crawl away from her
                                                  kicked in.

Landbound, you learned lines, steps, a solid geometry
beyond her grasp. Now you think she has nothing to say
to you, nodding dumbly under your flint-edged
questions.

Listen: your heart remembers the language of water,
the salt swells of joy or sorrow rise and overrun
your eye's thin coastline. She moves you to join in duet,

and the hum that accompanies her playing pours from
the throat of the dream that will lift you past the sea-wall,
beyond the cadences of time, its island patois.

Lieutenant Love
— in memory of Professor C.C. Love, 1911-1998

1.

Only those who hadn't sailed on both seas
  might have viewed his move from the Atlantic
    to the poetic as a change in course.

For him, escorting minds through the black straits
  that divide a book's white-shored expanses
    ran currents he knew from convoy duty —

asked the old willingness to abandon
  foothold for rolling freefall, taxed the same
    ear for the rhythm of what lay hidden

in holds beneath familiar rhythms:
  throat-sound under the gearwheel's pitch, breath caught
    in pockets where cogs were missing, muscle-

spasm blipping the scanned line's steady note.
  Defenceless small craft in his charge once more
    sailed through basics (not to launch out full-lit,

not full-speed into the self's mined harbour)
and headed well beyond the textbook runs
by trusting instinct over instrument.

2.

Was Yeats's "Sailing to Byzantium"
    his favourite because it also made
        song one with sailing, or because its dreamt

voyage made light of monumental shade?
    Though his square-chiselled shoulders might have thrown
        shadows on a corvette's bridge or towered

over a classroom desk, all his commands
    took the first-person plural, semaphores
        whose workings called forth the community

they spelled. Captaining, he could level fierce
    depth charges where the ego rode concealed
        to menace a sea lane's peaceful commerce,

yet much preferred the navigator's role.
    Translating lines and figures into tack
        and anchorage, watching the green hills build

from an unfurled flat map's watery wake,
    he made a calling of his wartime rank,
        a "place-holder" whose place no one could take.

3.
He had absorbed the sea's teachings. His step
   questioned the firmness of dry land, knees flexed
   for shift or letdown, yet he accepted

the trade-off, yielded sureness in exchange
   for buoyancy (some Viking sea-raider
   ancestor surfacing in that reflex),

He knew that — whether on water or earth —
   all merely outer passages will founder
   in papery shallows; that a wordbound

wide-margined country's most alluring ports
   can never harbour what, once human, lives
   "out of nature" in our songs and stories.

The steersman of full-sailed imaginings
   looks back and guides us through those inland waters
   whose depths he sounded in his twin callings.

Keeps our course true, teaches — in all its weathers —
   the hidden mortal currents of the heart
   where love is the only navigator.

What We Owe the Stars

1.

We must start lower, with what we owe the boulder:
debt-burden, heaped silt sloughed from the floods of many
generations. We tote it up by climbing back

into our mothers' bodies, as they into theirs
hitching a ride on the chain drawn back in through them
to the stone age where sedimented sand began

to impart its lessons in patience. In return,
since we are still too skittish to repay in kind,
we will feel the warmth it can't when the sun bathes it.

2.

Nor will our debt to water ever be discharged
no matter how much we give back to the oceans
of what we take from the rain, for we embezzle

at all its ports of call. Eyes loot the waterfall's
downcast face, and siphoning mouths mime in reverse
fountain's overpayment to basin. Only, when

water teeters mutely at a cup's lip, our lips
can part and, on the brim of our utmost plunder,
give its insatiable soul a voice in our "aah."

3.

We owe most to the stars who, possessing neither
stone's unwavering bastions nor water's slippery
cape of invisibility, have soldiered deep

into death's cold country, diminutive cadets
each holding only a small candle for defence.
We owe it to them to love each other and launch

our blood-warmed breath to secure their farthest outposts:
then the stars will stop shivering with loneliness
and the night will close its eyes on sleep like a stone.

Acknowledgements

Early versions of some of these pieces, sometimes with different titles, appeared in *ARC*, *Canadian Literature*, *The Fiddlehead*, *Grain*, *The Malahat Review*, *The New Quarterly*, *The Southern Review*, and *Southwest Review*, and also in *In Fine Form: The Canadian Book of Form Poetry*, ed. Kate Braid and Sandy Shreve (Polestar, 2005) and *Poetry and Liturgy*, ed. Margo Swiss (St. Thomas Press, 2006). Warm thanks to all the editors for their continuing interest and encouragement.

I am also very grateful to the staff of Goose Lane Editions for their superlative help in turning this collection into a book. Special thanks go to Laurel Boone, Sabine Campbell, Lisa Rousseau, Brenda Berry, and Julie Scriver for invaluable contributions.

These poems have gained much from the kind but keen critical attention shown by a number of friends and fellow poets. Foremost is Don McKay, whose editing of the collection for Goose Lane was characteristically inspired and stimulating. There's hardly a poem in the book that hasn't benefited from his engagement with it; I owe much to him for his enthusiasm, for his vision of the whole, and for innumerable detailed suggestions. He, Roo Borson, and Maureen Scott Harris are the primary inspiration behind the poems in the fourth section: I had originally thought of acknowledging this by dedicating individual poems to them, but their influence is too extensive and too interwoven for that approach to be just. The same is true of Ross Leckie, devoted friend, kindred spirit, and guiding presence, whose wisdom and kindness know no bounds. Also, as ever, members of the Vic writing group have been of great help, particularly this time Allan Briesmaster, Al Moritz, and Leif Vaage. And finally, I want to express my gratitude most emphatically to my "in-house" readers, Bert Almon (who may live in Edmonton but who is a constant welcome presence thanks to email) and above all my wife, Julie, for providing invaluable responses to virtually every draft of every poem.

John Reibetanz was born in New York City, grew up in the eastern United States and Canada, and put himself through university by working at numerous unpoetic jobs; he is probably the only member of the League of Canadian Poets to have belonged to the Amalgamated Meatcutters Union. A finalist for both the National Magazine Awards and the National Poetry Competition, he has given poetry readings in Canada and the United States. His poems have appeared in journals including *Poetry* (Chicago), *The Paris Review*, *Canadian Literature*, *The Malahat Review*, *The Fiddlehead*, *The Southern Review*, and *Quarry*. In 2003 he was awarded first prize in the international Petra Kenney Poetry Competition, and his fifth collection, *Mining for Sun*, was shortlisted for the ReLit Poetry Award.

John Reibetanz teaches English at Victoria College, University of Toronto, where he received the first Victoria University Teaching Award. In addition to poetry, he has written essays on Elizabethan drama and on modern and contemporary poetry, as well as a book on *King Lear* and translations of modern German poetry.